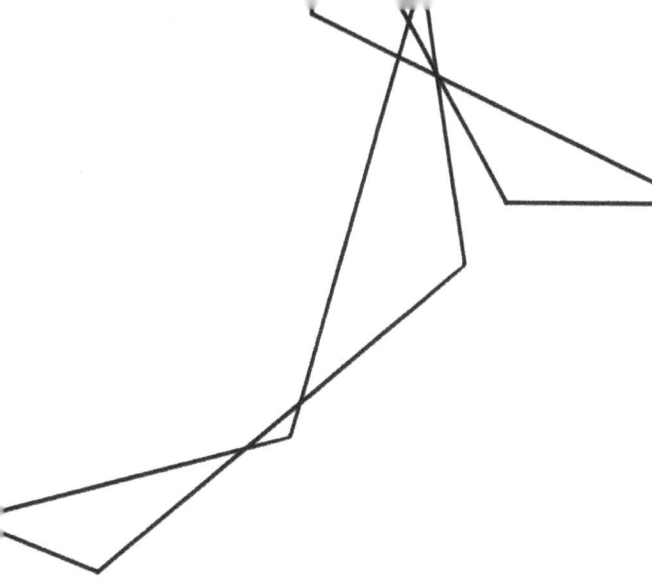

LETTERS TO MY LOVERS

Mae Rennoe

Text copyright © Mae Rennoe 2023
Design copyright© Chrissie Yeomans 2023
All rights reserved.

Mae Rennoe has asserted her right under the Copyright, Designs and Patents Act 1988 to be identified as the author of this work.

This title is intended for the enjoyment of adults, and is not recommended for children due to the mature content it contains.

No part of this book may be reprinted or reproduced or utilised in any form or by electronic, mechanical or any other means, now known or hereafter invented, including photocopying or recording, or in any information storage or retrieval system, without the permission in writing from the Publisher and Author.

First published 2022
by Rowanvale Books Ltd
The Gate
Keppoch Street
Roath
Cardiff
CF24 3JW
www.rowanvalebooks.com

A CIP catalogue record for this book is available from the British Library.
ISBN: 978-1-914422-18-8

*To everyone who helped me turn these words
into more than scribbles in a notebook,
thank you for the push.*

Dear Lovers,

I am a mirror for your love.
You cannot love me if you hate what I reflect,
and so your affection is conversion therapy.
Break me down and hope for diamonds—
but clutch me close and find
I am no more than broken glass.

Dear Kisses,

First,
you were sudden.
Innocent.
Not supposed to happen.
But I didn't run.

Second, you were stolen unexpectedly.
I was impressionable and lost, and you could have led me away with your affections.
But you only wanted to be seen by someone. Anyone.
So nearly a year later I am still calling your house.
Your relationship with my best friend long over.
I talk to your dad with warmth and ask for YOU.
Not the tough-guy nickname with goth makeup and biker jewellery by which you are known.
I ask for Eric, my friend, who is sad and lonely, warm and accepting, and who likes the girl I learned to never show. The girl I learned to protect.
It doesn't matter that we never spent feverish moments entangled.
For one year, your spirit loved mine. It meant the world.

To the torch in the darkness. You never
should have happened.
Your lips were unbearably soft.
Torn between drowning and parched, cotton
mouth dry from long neglect of tenderness,
I gasped for breath, caught in a riptide of
your adoration.

Letters To My Lovers

Dear Almosts,

Not quite lovers,
from a distance—   pen pals of a sort.
We have never folded ourselves into each other's arms,
but the embrace of your beautifully brilliant and oh so tortured mind
still warms me like a warm wood stove when I pause to remember you.

Mr Bumblebee,
I admire how you appreciate every flower you see.
But without a queen, come winter where will you be?

Sir Cardinal, you wear my weight in tattoo ink and gold—
but you're no tough guy, no thug, don't think I'm fooled.
I respect your commitment to the animal kingdom,
am content with red tips while you flaunt your crimson.

Mae Rennoe

Dear Addict,

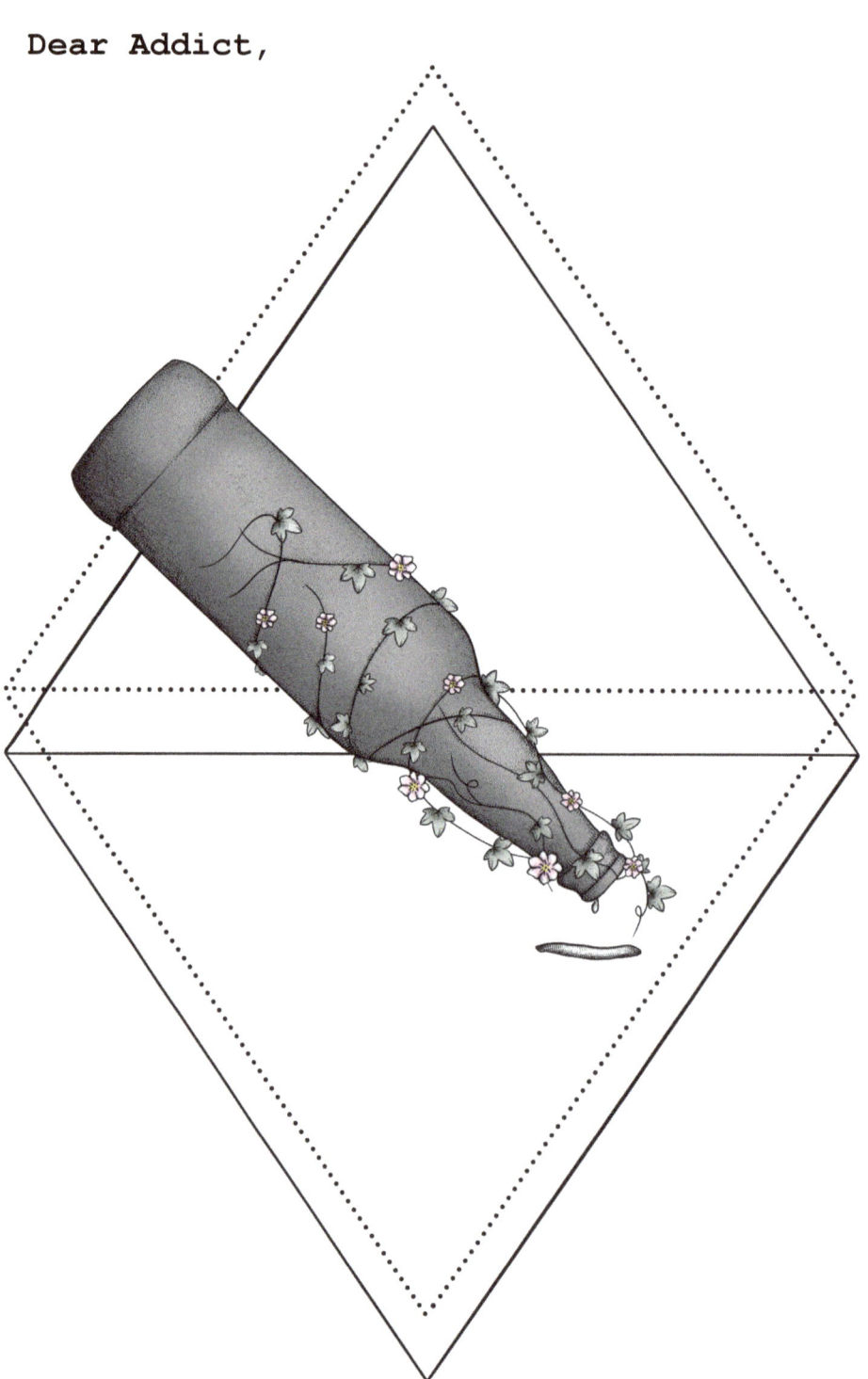

You were a twilight child and I so adored
the goofy sober grin that dimmed shadows
never quite erased.
Born to sunshine and raised in darkness.
Like Hades and Persephone—you led me through
the land of dusk.
I learned to love it there. Even more than I
loved you.

I love you.

Three words to make me shudder,

three words to make me run.

Coincidentally, three is the number of fights you tried to pick at the bar tonight.

Two is the number of times you cornered me and tried to steal

three words that should always be a gift.

One is the number of opportunities we have to say 'I love you' for the very first time.

We pull up at the house and your best friend turns his head as I bail from the car because he doesn't want to watch this scene unfold.

The smokers I live with go in the house because they have already seen this movie too many times.

I intend to stomp inside and slam the door—a grand exit on your behaviour,

but you jerk me around to face you and your hands are manacles around my wrists.

I try to pull away but your grip promises no escape.

You are sorry.

Tonight won't happen again.

You love me.

You're sorry.

I tell you I don't want to talk anymore.

I tell you to let me go and you say NO

and in the adrenaline of the moment my mind fills with wonder.

I am wondering if I will have bruises tomorrow,

as you make it clear that the only way to gain my freedom is with three words you are desperate to hear.

I am wondering why nobody is helping me escape.

Dear 'Tough Guy',

                                      Dear 'Nice Guy',

from the wrong side of the tracks.

                from the wholesome part of town.

Your 'I love you'—

                                Your 'I love you'—

tastes like Alpine…

                        tastes like Moosehead…

Feels like being psychically restrained—no path of escape.

I felt akin to a bug under a microscope
next to your constant accusations of
infidelity.
Suspicion and jealousy rode tandem
behind anyone who was not yourself.
Your anger reigned supreme.
Now I can't help but notice…
How little time you needed
to find a new object of distrust.

Sobriety looks good on you.

I only got to witness it once.
After a fight. A silence. A hospital stay.
Ultimatums from myself.

You showed concern about my academic probation.
You sat and conversed calmly;
no anxious jitters to make you restless.
You were sweet, goofy—
more secure in your own skin
as you basked in my laughter.
You held my hand on a skating rink.

You couldn't maintain it,
and the next girl made you worse.

But the girl after straightened you out.
You wanted a better father for her than you had for yourself.
She looks like the girl you left me for,
but she has your eyes and that goofy smile I adore.

There are five of those smiles in your family photos when I creep.
Four on little ladies and one on their daddy,
who can only wear the expression when he is Sober.

Sobriety looks good on you.

Mae Rennoe

Dear Tall Glass of Whiskey,

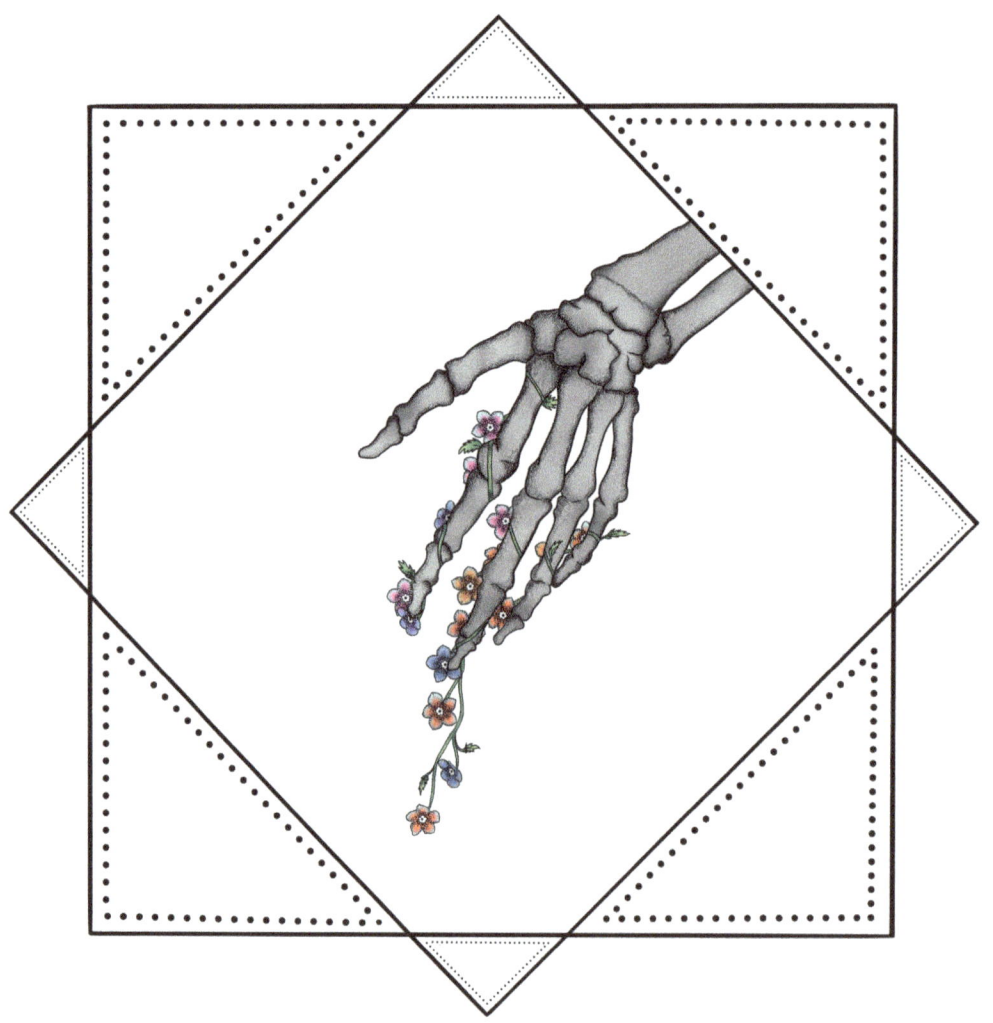

I want to compare

your love

and its consequences
to some natural disaster
like a tornado
or a hurricane,
and in truth

I overflowed

with your love
like a stream in flood.
Just like water
your affections

eroded me

unseen.

So when your love receded
the damage
was long done,
and in the aftermath
I carried on
like the caves
worn into coastal cliff faces,

empty

save for barnacles of sadness
and seaweed of despair.
The only thing
that filled the gaping hole
left in your wake
was crashing waves

of anger.

Which only served
to further the destruction
of my fractured psyche.

My dreams have turned to nightmares once again.
I dream of the terror he inflicted,
but in the dreams he wears your face. A face I used to love.
From it are your blue eyes gazing back at me.

Why must you be—   *resurrected*

every time I lay you to rest?

I felt blossoms grow when you reached into my heart,
and when I looked in the mirror I saw an inner glow.
A secret goddess I hadn't seen before,
but then the blossoms bloomed the brown of dried blood and rusty razor edges.
The glow beneath my skin remained on the next glance in the mirror
and there she was—the goddess, of denial.
So I have been drowning your garden all these years,
with tears—to ruin the petals.
I scoured the goddess with self-loathing,
and in my resolve to destroy your garden I discovered that I have washed the petals a beautiful black, with sharp clean edges.
And the goddess looking back in the mirror is not a fragment of light, but a moonbeam in an ever-darkening night. A goddess ready to fight.

Mae Rennoe

Dear Lovers,

I keep looking at all the yous—
staring back at me from the rearview mirror.

Who wanted me more than anything else—
With your offerings of peace-coated manipulation,

and hands that could make me tremble by turns with lust and fear.

All worshipped me—none *enough*.
Yet tried convincing me it was *myself* who was not enough.

Mae Rennoe

Dear Committed,

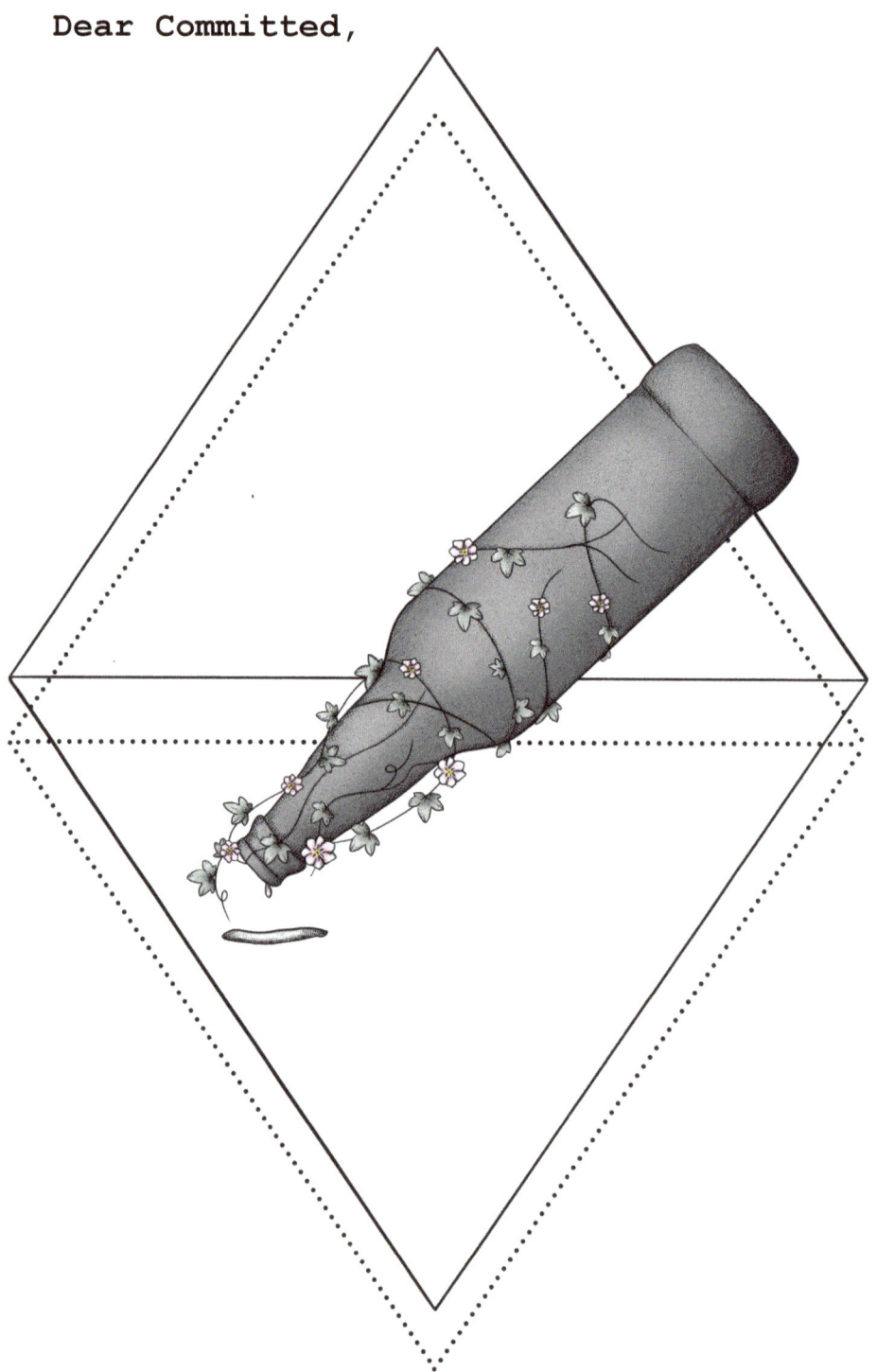

You love an idea. The idea of me.
A vision in which I adore
your cantankerous, insensitive ways,
and dote on your every repressed then
inappropriately expressed macho feeling
from behind a carefully made face framed by
sleek straight mid-length hair.
I am not and do not care to be her.
I am naked-faced and frequently appalled by
what emerges from your mouth.
I will not dote on your demons. Nor empty my soul—
to fill your imaginary box.

Your love is a prison.
Inside the electrified barbed wire fence and
cement walls of your heart,
the dream you have for us is a dream in
which I live by another's rules.
My days—
scheduled according to your wishes.
My hair, hygiene, attire—
shaped at your indulgence.
A heart should be:
a guest room, a home, a safe place to rest.
So why does yours feel like a cage?

Dear 'Nice Guy',

                                  Dear 'Tough Guy',

from the wholesome part of town.

              from the wrong side of the tracks.

Your 'I love you'—

                              Your 'I love you'—

tastes like Moosehead…

                                tastes like Alpine…

Feels like being psychically restrained—no path of escape.

You are a man with flaws and hopes and dreams, and you think you love me.

But every time I try to build a life with you, the home you dream of is a box, and I am not a cube or even a square.

I am a halogen lightbulb. My mother taught me not to shine for the wrong socket.

She regrets it now that I am 27 and unmarried, 27 and childless.

But I am glad she taught me strength because when you hand me a box and ask me for more, the answer is no.

You want more, but only inside that box that feels like a cage; and only more for you.

Because if I am more for myself, then I might be more for everyone, and you are not secure enough in your masculinity to accept that traces of my light might shine into hearts that aren't yours.

The answer is no because you WANT to love me, but only the pretty little picture of me that dances in your head, blinding you to the real woman standing before you.

You don't want to grow and live and BE with me, you want to own me.

So, instead, you have lost me.

Dear Self-Assured,

Who thinks to achieve another girl-next-door beauty with the classic neg,
you deliver a barrage of rapid-fire questions to see if I am worthy of a place on your roster,

>>> as if I would ever consider such a thing at all.

Learn a new trick.

Without your innuendo I am aware that you are a man with a man's desires.

Honey, take care to heed the story of the Turtle and the Hare;
don't blow your running start by sleeping on my intellect.

As one passably pretty with a great ass, you act as if I am no more than a pleasing option, and while I hold fully to the practice of knowing one's own self-worth—

Never forget you were gifted with the miracle of mitochondrial DNA,
but I was bestowed with the gift of GIVING it.

Letters To My Lovers

Dear Lighthouse,

Please.
Allow yourself,
give yourself permission,
to feel what must be felt.
Your enlightenment does not protect you from
society's influence.
Lay down with your hurt.
Embrace your depression.
Be overwhelmed and process the burden
without searching for its root in some
physiological ailment.
Acknowledge—
that sometimes men struggle to swim.
And fewer men after you will *drown*.

Our secret garden was supposed to allow me the
freedom to peer into other kinds of flowers.
Instead I see that you are just a man
and cannot help but want to keep your
pollinators to yourself.
You're posting photos of date night with
someone who isn't me while getting pouty over
my evening reconnecting with an old friend.
This grooming doesn't work on a woman wise
to the ways of control.
Every time you overstep, I erect another
wall between myself and you.

I poured poison into you and you drank it like wine.
I thought you were a lighthouse in the storm, but you were a lantern in the darkness—

        and I, the hapless mesmerised moth.

So tell me why one glance from you has me yearning, has me fluttering,
while my wings are still raw from your last embrace?

Dear Inquisitive,

There is no mistaking the way you look at me.
Your eyes ask mine:
Are you attainable?
Are you a possibility?
Am I?
I have no answer.

It all comes to a head with a question.
Do I want to do something?
I don't know, but I will anyway.
Somehow this business of breaking hearts becomes easier the more fractured mine becomes.

Dear Moral High Ground,

You are the steady rushing of a river.
Flowing over the same path for so long that
you wear yourself into mountains.
I turned myself into a fantasy, but you
wanted conventional and modern.
For a moment I think all that water
is enough for me
until I can taste your moan but you can't
hear the climax in my hands.
And I remember, I am as raindrops falling
from the sky.
You are too easily wavered by my hurricanes
and droughts,

   I—   I think it takes an ocean…

Mae Rennoe

Dear Lovers,

The love long unrequited,
'The Rose That Grew from Concrete'. Twice bought, twice gifted, and both of you have left. With no backward glance. Once more I buy this book. The third—the last. For the love affair I should have had. The one that's with myself.

Mae Rennoe

Dear Smoke and Mirrors,

We look at ourselves:
    see jagged bloody piles of ground glass.
We look at each other:
    see the beautiful stained-glass mosaics
    of a church.

You reach for me with a soul that frightens you
but hands that already know what they wish to do.
So kiss me.
Like it makes your knees weak.
It might be enough.

Presenting cool and calm,
your eyes betray a drowning man
lost on the high tides of despair—
reaching for me like one seeking dry land.
Thank you for reminding me that I am a siren
with the power to place you back on shore.
Be brave, take my hand, drowning man.

You've been running from the fires you set—
while I play chicken with my own.
You saw me by the way and stopped.
Someone should have warned you that I love
the burn.

Rooted in famine like I—
you are all vibrant hazard;
rare blossoms, and sticky-sweet, corrosive
juices.
For the first time I don't feel like too much.
You love me for my savagery,
as you love me for my softness.

I am a shore of shattered glass
silently waiting for you to slice open on me.
Instead I soften—little by little—
beneath each wave of your gentle sea.

Hanging by a thread under a burning sun,
gripping the edges of a black yawning chasm with waning will.
From the far edges I can hear the people who are supposed to love you yelling,
'How could you? Just climb up and stop fucking around.'
But the edges are still caving in and they don't seem to care.
When I reach for you with moonlight, you shrink away—afraid I'll take the same tumble.
But Love, can't you see? I am already a ghost.

I am weak over words.
Enthralled and terrified I suffocate—
on my own inhalations.
Too weak—
to breathe life
into three words you need to hear.

By night you write your eulogy,
as by day you dance with your ghosts.
Watching you dig your own grave
is my worst nightmare.

I have spent a lifetime shrinking.
The shadow for every sun, and the dark for every moon.
But there is no hiding next to you, who are more star than sun.
Glittering in the night. If I want you, I must glimmer too…

I told you I loved you at the edge of that caprice.
Hoping in vain that it would keep you warm after I forced you to look
into hollow eyes, at a cold unreachable soul.
I told you I loved you, hoping against hope that you would stay.

Truth or lies? You 'confess'
your fear of stepping close,
of basking in my glow.
Alright, it's fine.
Worship from afar.
Never forget the goddess is only touchable
in her most ordinary form.

I flinched before the golden gleam
of a shining warrior.
But you are soft. soft. soft.
You glow for me.
A gentle beacon in the dark.
The iridescent shimmer of a fallen angel.
And the twilight hour soothes my wary soul.

They say love shouldn't hurt.
But I love you so much—it hurts.
Like I'm so full I'm tearing apart
at rough-sewn seams
left over from the last time I overflowed.

The boy is still more smoke than sparkle.
I lust for the smoke and I long for the
sparkle.

Author Profile

Raised on a small farm in rural Canada, Mae shared a passion for reading and writing with her beloved Grandfather. Those memories now inspire Mae's deep love of writing and motivation to pursue their shared dream.

https://mrennoe.blogspot.com

https://www.instagram.com/maerennoe/

Publisher Information

Rowanvale Books provides publishing services to independent authors, writers and poets all over the globe. We deliver a personal, honest and efficient service that allows authors to see their work published, while remaining in control of the process and retaining their creativity. By making publishing services available to authors in a cost-effective and ethical way, we at Rowanvale Books hope to ensure that the local, national and international community benefits from a steady stream of good quality literature.

For more information about us, our authors or our publications, please get in touch.

www.rowanvalebooks.com
info@rowanvalebooks.com

Lightning Source UK Ltd.
Milton Keynes UK
UKHW050450160223
417096UK00030B/510